*What They Are Saying A*

"*A riveting piece of historical fiction, very much highly recommended reading.*" – **Midwest Book Review**

"*It is a book that I think could have the impact of a Gone With the Wind.*" – **Jonathan A. Noyalas, Assistant Professor of History and Director for Civil War Studies, Lord Fairfax Community College**

"*I think it is the best Civil War fiction book since Cold Mountain.*" – **James D. Bibb, Sons of Confederate Veterans, Trimble Camp 1836**

"*Not since reading Gone with the Wind have I enjoyed a book so much!*" – **Sarah Winch**

"*Andrea and Alex will surely take the place in my heart of Rhett and Scarlett as the perfect Civil War fictional love story!*" – **Angel Deyarmin**

"*A classic love story as much as it is a war story.*" – **Civil War Book Review**

## Books Available by Jessica James:

Above and Beyond: A Novel of the Civil War
*Finalist in 2013 USA Best Books Awards*

Noble Cause: A Novel of Love and War
*Winner of the John Esten Cooke Award for Southern Fiction*

Shades of Gray: A Novel of the Civil War in Virginia
*Winner of the Next Generation Indie Award for Regional Fiction*

### Other Literary Awards

2012 Bronze winner Foreword Magazine Book of the Year in Romance
2011 USA "Best Books 2011" Finalist in Historical Fiction
2011 Next Generation Indie Award for Best Regional Fiction
2011 Next Generation Indie Finalist in Romance category
2011 Next Generation Indie Finalist in Historical Fiction category
2011 NABE Pinnacle Book Achievement Award
2010 Stars and Flags: Second place for Historical Fiction
2009 HOLT Medallion Finalist for Best Southern Theme
2008 Indie Next Generation Finalist for Best Historical Fiction
2008 IPPY Award for Best Regional Fiction
2008 ForeWord Magazine Finalist for Book of the Year in Romance

# The Gray Ghost of Civil War Virginia

*John Singleton Mosby*

*By Jessica James*

# The Gray Ghost of Civil War Virginia

*John Singleton Mosby*

A Non-Fiction Companion to Jessica James'
Historical Fiction Novel
*Noble Cause*
(Originally titled *Shades of Gray*)

Cover Art Courtesy of John Paul Strain
"Fire in the Valley"
http://www.johnpaulstrain.com

*To Glenn who introduced me to the Gray Ghost and helped me walk in his footsteps.*

*"Our poor country has fallen a prey to the conqueror. The noblest cause ever defended by the sword is lost."*

*– John Singleton Mosby*

## PREFACE

*"To those of us whose experiences cover that period, memory brings back 'the tender grace of the days that are dead.' We must trust those of the rising generation to imagine that atmosphere of romance and chivalry which then pervaded the land, and in which only were possible the deeds which I shall attempt to recount."*
**– John Alexander, *Mosby's Men***

It always makes me smile when Civil War "historians" and professors of history attempt to explain to me—a historical fiction author—that the "romance" of the Civil War never existed... that the chivalry, gallantry and courage of the men of the South are only a myth.

That's interesting, considering the above quote and thousands of similar narratives that can be found in diaries, memoirs, newspaper clipping and books written in the 1860s. Why the "scholars" discount them or pretend they do not exist escapes me.

In any event, this book on John Singleton Mosby is not written for historians, nor is it meant to serve as a history of his command. It is intended only as a brief introduction for the readers of my historical fiction novels who wish to learn more about the man that my main character, Colonel Alexander Hunter, is based upon.

As you will see, there is no lack of material on this iconic Civil War figure. In addition to Mosby's own wartime *Reminiscences*, there are numerous volumes written on Mosby's Civil War exploits—at least half a dozen of them written by his own men shortly after the war.

Although there are reprints available of many of these books, I'm sure that most historical fiction readers are not interested in tracking them down—let alone wading through the military tactics and expeditions that many of them include. For that reason, I have attempted to gather some of the most pertinent facts, and weave them together with a few of the more interesting stories and raids they describe. I think you will agree they are unlike anything you've read about the Civil War heretofore.

The first thing you may notice that set Mosby and his men apart from others is that they operated independently—and usually in the enemy's rear as opposed to its front. The unit's primary objectives were to destroy railroad supply lines, intercept dispatches, and basically harass any Federal troops that dared stray into their territory.

This book only touches the surface of the bold, daring—and sometimes humorous—episodes recounted in the memoirs of Mosby's men after the Civil War. For every anecdote of romance, intrigue and adventure included here, there are dozens of others that were not, but I hope this glimpse will inspire you to want to learn more.

For instance, readers who are familiar with Mosby will notice that his greatest—or at least his most well-known feat of kidnapping a Union general from his bed, only receives a brief mention in this book. Though it is certainly an achievement unsurpassed during the Civil War, it is one that can be found quite easily in an Internet search. I chose instead to relate some of the lesser-known tales that carry with them all of the romance and intrigue that drew me to Mosby in the first place.

JOHN S. MOSBY

Likewise, this book doesn't include skirmishes in which Mosby's men lost. Yes, there were a few of those instances, and they were very costly. Nor does it include Mosby getting shot (more than once), or the hanging of some of his men by General Custer, or details on his pre- or post-war life. It is my hope that the reader will take advantage of the resources I list at the end of the book to learn more if they are so inclined.

For some background, I learned about Mosby when I moved to Virginia fresh out of college in the 1980s. Little did I know what an influence this chivalrous Confederate officer would have on my life way back then! As an equine veterinary technician working a dream job at a state-of-the-art horse hospital, I had little interest in the Civil War—or writing for that matter.

But as fate would have it, this enterprising cavalryman drew me into the clutches of the past and never let go. As I began to read about his dauntless and daring rides across the same hills I passed on my way to work each day, I started writing down snippets of story lines about a similar band of gallant outlaws.

You can probably picture them as vividly as I did when I wrote: *All were bronzed by exposure, and marked with the vigilance that is born of dangerous duty. Like other Confederate cavalry units, the men looked as if they had been born in their saddles—likewise like they were perfectly willing to die there.*

So began my new career as a writer of Civil War fiction, an occupation that has led to awards and publishing success—all because of an infatuation with a man they called the Gray Ghost.

After reading this book, I think you will agree that Colonel Alexander Hunter's fictional expeditions in my Civil War novels are tame compared to those of Mosby and his men. They say that truth is stranger than fiction—and surely where Mosby is concerned that is a fact.

But despite his intrepidness on the battlefield and his reputation for courage and valor, Mosby's war-time letters to his wife show a softer side. They always began with, "Dearest Pauline," and ended with "Kiss my babes for me," or "Don't let my precious ones forget me." (His wife died after giving birth to their eighth child in 1876. Mosby was 43 years old and never remarried).

In closing, I'll let one of Mosby's youngest recruits, John Munson, describe a slice of his life as told in his book *Reminiscences of a Mosby Guerilla.*

*"I have returned with him [Mosby] from a raid that covered two or three days of almost constant riding, only to be told to get ready to start on another expedition at once. In such cases we would take a hurried bath, put on clean clothes, get a fresh horse from the stable, pocket a few extra cartridges, eat something if it was ready, and gallop away. I used to think it was glorious sport in those days. Every affair in which Mosby and his men figured had in it something novel, something romantic, something which is worth the telling..."*

Dear reader, I hope you agree. Enjoy the ride!

*Jessica James*

## INTRODUCTION

N o name in the annals of the Civil War conjures up a more gallant, romantic and awe-inspiring image than that of Confederate Colonel John Singleton Mosby of Virginia.

The epitome of the Southern cavalier, Colonel Mosby was a charismatic officer whose small band of partisans outwitted and outfought the Union army on the fields and farmlands of northern Virginia. So great was the panic inspired by this one officer's military ingenuity, so prominent was the threat he created to the Union forces, that he came to be known in the north as more of a myth than a man.

Starting with just nine cavalrymen on detached duty from the command of General James Ewell Brown (JEB) Stuart in early January 1863, Mosby's unit eventually grew into one of the most feared and fast-hitting cavalry groups in the Confederacy.

As a result of the panic he instilled and the reputation that he secured, the area stretching from the Potomac River to the Shenandoah Valley became known as Mosby's Confederacy during the War Between the States. And today, as a tribute to that brave Virginian and his loyal band of followers, the region is known as the Mosby Heritage Area.

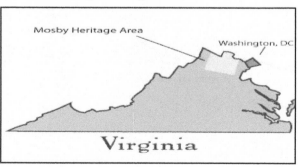

# Map of Mosby's Confederacy in Virginia

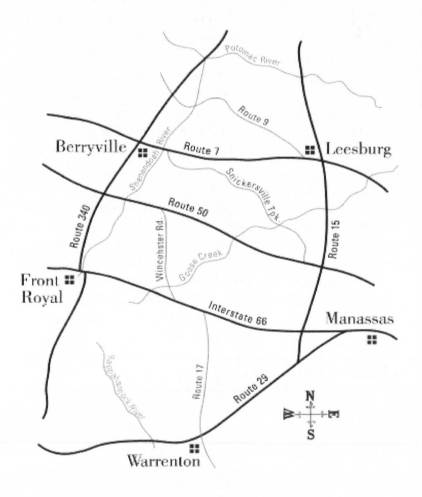

## THE LEGEND

Mosby's historic legacy survives to this day because the success of his exploits as a partisan ranger during the American Civil War have never been surpassed—or really even rivaled—in military history.

With fewer than 400 men at any one time (although more than 1,000 were on the rolls by the end of the war), he often fought more than three times his own strength, relying more heavily on boldness and bluff than actual fighting power. His command suffered about 640 casualties during his two-year partisan career, while killing, wounding or capturing at least 2,900 of the enemy.

According to war records, the Union army dispatched more than 70 different missions with the sole intent of eradicating Mosby's band. This played right into the hands of the rebel commander's ultimate goal, which was to divert as many of the enemy's troops as possible from the front lines to guard and protect their rear from attack.

As Mosby states in a report to General (J.E.B.) Stuart in September of 1863, "The military value of the species of warfare I am waging is not to be measured by the number of prisoners and material of war captured from the enemy, but by the heavy details it compels him to make in order to guard his communications."

His success is in the numbers, as historical records show he diverted as many as fifteen times his own strength for a single battle, and sidetracked 1,800 infantry from the Battle of Third Winchester and Fisher's Hill alone.

But the diversion of Federal troops was not Mosby's only contribution to the Southern cause. During the course of his illustrious career, Mosby and his men captured more than 3,500 horses and mules, a significant contribution to the Confederacy considering its constant shortage of this valuable commodity.

In response to those who suggest it was as much his officers as Mosby himself that accounted for his successes, Mosby Ranger John Alexander says in his book *Mosby's Men*: "The truth is that Mosby conceived a plan of warfare, sought and found a favorable theater, attracted and made the most of suitable men, and with them worked out his conception to glorious results."

## IN THE BEGINNING

When the Civil War began, John Mosby had no military training. Making a living as a lawyer in Bristol, Va., he, like many other Virginians, opposed secession. However, once President Abraham Lincoln called for 75,000 troops to fight against the Southern states, Virginia seceded and Mosby joined the military saying, *Virginia is my mother. God bless her! I cannot fight against my mother can I?*

Mosby began his military career as a private, performing all of the mundane tasks that military requires, including that scourge that all soldiers detest: picket duty. In the spring of 1863, General JEB Stuart took a chance on the young soldier by giving him a few men with the simple order to "harass the enemy."

After returning from one of his first expeditions with a captured Union general, two captains, 30 privates and 58 horses, Mosby's career as a partisan ranger was sealed. He accomplished this extraordinary feat with only 29 men, riding into a well-fortified, Federally-occupied town and taking the prisoners without losing a man—or firing a shot.

Virgil Carrington Jones summarizes the expedition in his book *Ranger Mosby:* "Twenty-nine men behind a bold leader had wormed their way through strong picket lines to the very point where enemy officers slept, yanked them out of bed, laughed at the guards on their way past, and disappeared ahead of the rising sun."

Mosby used as his model the Revolutionary War General Francis Marion. Success in this type of warfare depends on accurate reconnaissance, which required Mosby to find and use the best scouts—usually local men familiar with every road and path in the region where he operated.

He also scouted himself before deciding whether or not to attack, but seldom asked for advice or took anyone in his confidence. Even his most trusted officers were not informed of the intent of a raid or the size of the opposing force until their orders were given at the point of attack. All who followed him, followed without fear, trusting him implicitly with their lives.

His men apparently did not mind following their leader blindly. John Munson wrote about his war experiences in the book *Reminiscences of a Mosby Guerrilla,* saying, "I do not remember ever hearing anybody ask Mosby where he was going or what his plans were."

Even when not on a raid, Mosby's restless mind seemed ever busy with details of battle plans, often causing him to retreat into periods of intense concentration as he worked out his strategy. During these instances, when he paced up and down or lapsed into a sullen silence, his men would withdraw and leave him undisturbed.

Munson, who often accompanied Mosby on scouts, recalled one expedition in which the two men trotted and galloped, boot-leg to boot-leg for twenty miles. "Not once did he look at me, nor one word did he utter in all that ride. I thought my tongue would become paralyzed from long disuse."

As Mosby's successes grew, so did the number of men in his command—from a few dozen when he first started out in 1863, to more than a thousand by the end of the war. As a result of his reputation and the accolades he received, some of his recruits were actually officers who resigned their positions in the regular army for the honor of serving under Mosby as privates.

Part of Mosby's allure was his freedom to act independently

under the Scott Partisan Ranger Law. This law authorized the formation of independent cavalry companies whose members would serve without pay and supply their own horses. In return, they were entitled to keep any spoil of war captured from the enemy.

Popular print of Colonel John S. Mosby by the late Michael Gnatek Jr.

"We were mounted, armed, and equipped entirely off the enemy," Mosby wrote in his *Memoirs*, "but, as we captured a great deal more than we could use, the surplus was sent to supply Lee's army."

This drew another segment of society to Mosby's command—men in the region who were capable of bearing arms, but who had chosen to remain on their farms rather than go off to fight. These men were more than willing to ride with Mosby now and then with the objective of securing a new horse or some harness. The regular Mosby Men called them "conglomerates" and Mosby once said that they resembled the Democrat party, being "held together only by the cohesive power of public plunder."

Along with the size of his command, Mosby's rank likewise rose steadily. He became a major in 1863, having been given permission to organize Company A of the 43rd Battalion of Virginia Cavalry on June 10 of that year. His final promotion was to the rank of colonel late in 1864.

Gen. Robert E. Lee cited Mosby for meritorious service more often than any other Confederate officer during the course of the war, and in one such communication said, "Hurrah for Mosby! I wish I had a hundred like him."

## A METHOD TO THE MADNESS

Mosby fought upon simple doctrines that his enemies could neither predict nor guard against. He was in their front, in their rear, on their flank—at one place one day and in another the next. Because of his unorthodox method of warfare he got the reputation of being a bushwhacker or guerilla. As Colonel George Gray of the 6th Michigan Cavalry reported after being ambushed twice on the same night, "Mosby did not fight fairly. He surprised me..."

His men, on the other hand, thought very highly of their leader. Dr. Aristides Monteiro wrote in his book *War Reminiscences by the Surgeon of Mosby's Command,* "I assert the belief that no man ever possessed a greater power of quick perception, or more promptness of thought and action, than did this meteoric genius of guerrilla warfare."

Indeed, Mosby's method was to throw aside the established rules of warfare, effectively using fear as his weapon of choice and surprise as his watchword. Thrust into a war, he had become a warrior, a leader who drove himself and everyone around him to seemingly impossible endeavors. With unceasing activity and always-unexpected movements, Mosby succeeded in keeping the enemy demoralized, because they never knew when to expect him—and terrorized because they never knew what to expect.

Despite his lack of military training, Mosby was a born leader who had somehow inherited the same sharp sense for his perilous business that a hound has for the trail of a fox. Intuitive at divining the intentions of the enemy, he likewise possessed an exceptional ability for attacking the unsuspecting, while avoiding those who were not. With seeming ease, he could deduce when to strike, where to strike and how to strike an overwhelming force—frequently and consistently with victorious results.

Shadowy figures on horseback staring down from the rolling hills of Virginia created panic in the Federal ranks below, because Union troops realized they were being watched, scrutinized and hunted by a cunning, tireless demon. It might be hours, or it might be days, but they could expect with certainty that the riders would eventually swoop down from the ridges, their talons sharpened and ready to seize their prey.

If not an all-out attack, the enemy could expect their pickets to mysteriously disappear, or wagons full of supplies to inexplicably go astray. Horses and mules were especially susceptible to vanishing into thin air, but ambulances, couriers, scouts—and even trains—were not safe in Mosby's territory.

Federal troops considered themselves stalked as unmercifully as a hungry lion hunts down its prey, learning the hard way what Mosby already knew—that the constant strain of watching, waiting and wondering when the ravenous beast was going to strike was as hard , if not harder on them, than fighting an outright battle.

But it was not only the element of surprise that drained the Federal's nerves. They were also perplexed with the speed with which the cavalrymen appeared, attacked—and then vanished. Like a bolt of lightning, the rebels would emerge with revolvers flashing, deal their deadly blow and then disappear, leaving nothing but the memory by the time the enemy could react. The silence and secrecy with which Mosby's men moved, the speed with which they attacked, and then eluded the enemy by scattering into the hills, kept Union forces always in doubt and forever in fear of these seemingly invincible assailants.

One of the reasons Mosby's men moved so stealthily is because they did not carry sabers, which could bang and clank against saddle fittings. However, noise was not the only reason that swords and sabres were prohibited from his command.

"I believe I was the first cavalry commander who discarded the sabre as useless and consigned it to museums for the preservation of antiquities," Mosby wrote after the war. "My men were as little impressed by a body of cavalry charging them with sabres as though they had been armed with cornstalks."

> "Revolvers in the hands of Mosby's men were as effective in surprise engagements as a whole line of ordnance in the hands of the enemy."
> – John Munson

Mosby's men were instead armed with at least two Colt revolvers of forty-four caliber. According to Munson, those who could afford it, or who had succeeded in capturing extra pistols, wore an extra pair in their saddle-holsters or stuck in their boot legs since there was little time to re-load during their quick-hit engagements.

"Revolvers in the hands of Mosby's men were as effective in surprise engagements as a whole line of ordnance in the hands of the enemy," Munson said. He also attributed their success to that fact that long and frequent practice had made every man a good shot, and that Mosby admonished his men never to fire a shot until the eyes of the other fellow were visible.

"It was no uncommon thing for one of our men to gallop by a tree at full tilt and put three bullets into its trunk in succession," Munson said. "This sort of shooting left the enemy with a good many empty saddles after an engagement."

## MOSBY IS EVERYWHERE

Mosby's innovative military strategy did not end with the elements of speed, surprise and fear. He further baffled the enemy by making his command appear massive and vast by using different detachments to hit more than one outpost in a single night. In this manner he succeeded in deluding the enemy of his own strength and whereabouts, for when they were looking for him or preparing for him in one place, he was attacking and creating havoc in another.

As a result, Mosby's command became so legendary, his reputation so menacing, his character so terrorizing, that the mere mention of his name struck fear in the hearts of the enemy. Stories were told and stretched and swelled until it became general gossip that Mosby's men appeared and disappeared with the mist; that when they arrived they made no sounds, and when they departed they left no tracks. Fear gave the stories a life of their own, and darkness and imagination multiplied the forces, until wild and mystical imaginations made him a supernatural terror.

There was no limit to Mosby's audacity in the minds of the enemy, and no end to his success. Consequently, when misfortune or disaster struck the Federals, no matter what the circumstances or who was responsible, the name whispered up and down the line was always the same: Mosby.

Of course, Mosby did nothing to lesson that sense of terror and dread. Calculating the importance of penetrating the enemy's mind with fear as valuable as penetrating his body with lead, he would occasionally carve his name in a nearby tree or sprawl it out in the dust of a captured camp. The significance of his method of warfare, after all, relied not so much on how many he actually engaged in fighting, but rather, how many he kept watching and guarding for that possibility.

As the months and years wore on, the great blue masses endeavored in vain to destroy the great chieftain and his fearless followers. Although they sent men by the thousands to eliminate him, their units would return greatly reduced in size, and always without their prize. Mosby repeatedly mystified, mortified and soundly routed Union forces in numbers vastly superior to his own—in more than one instance, killing and wounding more of the enemy than his own entire force combined.

Federal officers would bemoan their defeats, saying it could not be helped, the rebel chief and his band of demons were everywhere one moment and nowhere the next. Mosby's uncommon method of dispersing his men—meaning each man sought his own salvation in getting out of a tight spot— basically made it impossible for the Yankees to pursue. One minute the cavalrymen would be there en masse. The next they were scattered to the four winds.

Jones wrote in *Ranger Mosby:* "He lived and operated with the freedom of an independent commander believing that the fierce hostility the Federals displayed toward him was more on account of the sleep he made them lose than the number he killed and captured."

## ELUSIVE BANDIT

The unsuccessful excursions into Mosby's Confederacy eventually taught the Union troops what Mosby had always believed—that a large, well-armed, impeccably equipped force chasing a small group of horsemen on their native soil, was a bit like trying to catch a field mouse with a bear trap.

"As a line is only as strong as its weakest point, it was necessary for it to be stronger than I was at every point in order to resist my attacks," Mosby wrote. "It is easy, therefore, to see the great results that may be accomplished by a small body of cavalry moving rapidly from point to point on the communications of an army."

Consequently, over time, there came to be far less confidence in the success of any expeditions to find and destroy Mosby. In fact, the Yankees' strenuous efforts to rid the land of his little band resulted only in their own demoralization.

As a result, the officials in Washington tried to downplay Mosby's significance, hailing his command as nothing more than a roaming gang of guerrillas, bushwhackers and horse thieves. In truth they didn't know how to fight this mysterious opponent or his squad of elusive horsemen. They only knew that when he struck, the results were uneven and generally not in their favor.

Munson took the Yankees to task for the names they called Mosby's men. "Mosby's Men were not highwaymen, bushwhackers or ruffians and did not war upon any element other than that commonly recognized as the enemy," he wrote. "A very large percentage of them were well-bred, refined gentlemen and some of them had traveled widely. They regarded Mosby's Command as the proper channel through which to express their feelings on a subject that made action of some sort necessary."

Mosby, on the other hand, actually accepted the name of "bushwhacker." Not only is it a legitimate form of war, he wrote, but "it is just as fair and equally heroic to fire at an enemy from behind a bush as a breastwork or from the casemate of a fort."

**John Mosby, sitting center, with some of his men.**

## Mosby's 'Men'

Mosby, of course, did not attribute the success of his command to his own brilliant aptitude for battle, but rather on the fact that it was organized and permitted to operate in the Confederacy as a body of cavalry independent of the regular army.

Acting under the direct orders of General Stuart up to the time of Stuart's death, and then under General Lee, Mosby was so trusted by both officers that they permitted him to act on his own discretion. His mission was to annoy the enemy. How he did it, when he did it, and where he did it was left to his own ingenuity and devices.

Although these orders may seem vague to some, Mosby had a way of carrying them out with enthusiastic enterprise—and he had no scarcity of followers. Within a short period of time he had collected a conglomeration of high-souled sons of Virginia that, for all appearances, made it clear he had robbed the cradle and the grave in equal proportions. His "men" ranged in maturity from boys of but 15 summers to those well silvered over with the frost of age. (When he first began his command, he even recruited those convalescing at a nearby hospital).

But it was obvious from the appearance of his ranks that Mosby liked his youngest recruits the best. Mosby Ranger John Alexander explained, "Many of them were beardless boys, whose looks were far more suggestive of the nursery than of the war-path, and I fear that not all of them were model Sunday-school boys, either."

As he was among the youngest of Mosby's recruits, Alexander said that his fellow men were pleased to hear Mosby's commendation of them when asked why he allowed the youngsters to fight. "Why, they are the best soldiers I have," Mosby said. "They haven't sense enough to know danger when they see it, and will fight anything I tell them to."

It's not hard to imagine this jovial group appearing more like a band of rowdy school children than a force of ruthless warriors. Yet, Mosby knew, as the enemy did too, that they could fight as desperately as any set of men on earth. Though not one of them was a trained soldier, none of them had apparently needed much schooling on the subject. A high sense of honor and country served as the impelling principle of their service to the Confederacy—while the adventure and romance of serving with Mosby compelled them to fight like demons.

"One spirit of devil-may-care hilarity seemed to possess them all," Alexander said, reflecting on the ride to his first raid as a Mosby man. "The merry song, the jovial laughs rang out along the line, jest and joke followed amusing anecdotes; and now and then a group would bunch together to listen to some old veteran's tales."

Many of the men related in their after-war memoirs how Mosby would choose those who would be permitted to fight with his command. James Williamson perhaps described it the best, saying, "I have often watched him as he would stand intently gazing at a man—staring as though he were reading him through with those eyes, like a book, and then only removing his gaze as he walked off apparently satisfied with the result of his conclusion as to the man's worth or character."

Mosby apparently cared about character, but not background or social standing. His unit consisted of a wide assortment of men from every segment of Virginia society and culture—a mingling of traits, lineage and social status that bore out equally on the battlefield.

"Side by side rode the planter's son and the overseer's

boy; the banker dressed in soft officer's gray, and the poor adventurer whose suit of Union blue betrayed his dependence upon 'the spoils of the chase,'" Alexander wrote.

To the detractors who said the command was held together only by the cohesive power that comes from keeping the spoils of war, Alexander said, "The truth is that it was gathered, held together and shaped for its destiny by the personality of its leader."

**Some of Mosby's Rangers, with Mosby standing in center.**

## TREATED LIKE KINGS

As an independent command, Mosby's men were entitled to the legitimate spoil captured from the enemy and were immune to many of the military regulations that breed boredom and despair—no cooking detail, no military drilling, no monotonous camp life.

In fact, they had no regular camp, nor fixed quarters, nor tents. Their drilling, if you could call it such, consisted of horse racing and target shooting. Their training, for the most part, came from dear-bought experience of battle, and their military education was acquired in such a way no school could provide.

Truth be told, Mosby's men were not adept at pitching tents or cooking their own meals. Their headquarters was the saddle, where they were in frequent—sometimes almost constant—contact with the enemy. When on a raid or a scout they packed provisions for a day or three, at times entirely in their stomachs, and when allowed to rest, reposed under the great canopy of moon and stars, or sun and wind, or rain and snow, whatever the case would be.

Munson describes the motley crew and how they operated: "As a command, we had no knowledge of the first principles of cavalry drill, and could not have formed in a straight line had there ever been any need for our doing so. We did not know the bugle calls, and very rarely had roll-call. Our dress was not uniform in make or color; we did not address our officers, except Mosby, by their titles; in fact, we did not practice anything usually required of a soldier; and yet withal there was not another body of men in the army under better or more willing control of their leader."

He added, "Two things were impressed upon us well,

however: to obey orders and to fight."

When not in the saddle on active duty, Mosby's men protected themselves by disappearing into the homes of local families who were equally devoted to the cause of Southern independence. It was upon the generosity of these families that Mosby's cavaliers relied for meals, and, as a result, kings were not better fed nor more reverentially treated.

Those in the regular service grumbled about the life of the independents, who they claimed were far more familiar with picnicking than picketing and who, when not within the enemy's lines, had the ease of sleeping more often in the folds of a feather bed than in the cold embrace of Mother Earth.

That may have well been true. But in spite of the life of supposed comfort, the group assembled by Mosby was no less loyal, daring or determined then their comrades, and was, in fact, regarded by many as some of the best blood the South had to offer.

Dr. Monteiro describes how Mosby's men lived: "Our soldiers were quartered in squads of four to ten men at each private residence, mostly throughout the county of Fauquier (Virginia). When needed for action they were summoned by couriers to rendezvous at a given point. Within a few hours the entire command would always be ready for a raid."

But the Yankees soon caught on to this policy of protection, and began raiding the "safe" houses in the middle of the night. Monteiro notes how the men would get out of a tight spot: "Almost every dwelling occupied by Mosby's men was provided with trap-doors and other convenient subterranean hiding places. Whenever a house was attacked and surrounded by the enemy, a trap-door would immediately fly open, a few soldiers would disappear through the floor, a piece of carpet or oil-cloth would then be thrown carefully over the hiding place, after which a fierce search for rebels would be made in vain."

Another of Mosby's men, J. Marshall Crawford, recalled in the book *Mosby and His Men*, that when the Yankees were in the neighborhood, the partisans would take extra precautions.

"The boys built huts in the mountains, but would take their meals as heretofore, and after supper, or at dark, would repair with their horses to the huts, and repose as comfortably as in featherbeds. Some slept in caves in the mountains; some continued to remain as before, but had burrowed holes in the ground under the houses, which were entered through a trap-door."

Mosby, on the other hand, "with one or two of his staff, and often by himself, would generally, at dark, mount their horses, and go down to some good friend's house near the enemy's camps, and stay all night, thinking that the safest place," Crawford wrote.

As a reward for their esteemed service to the Old Dominion, Mosby made sure his men had the best mounts and finest arms the Union army could provide. Horses were chosen with reference to their speed, strength and endurance, with every man having at least two and Mosby having as many as six.

All of the horses in the command were kept well-nourished and well groomed, Mosby always careful to preserve the strength and vigor of horses between raids due to their heavy use on their excursions. No effort was deemed too large if it concerned the welfare of a horse, for they were as indispensable to the command, if not more so, as the soldiers themselves.

Alexander wrote, "Rough riders they were, as indeed they had need to be. For three or four hundred men to preserve their organization for years in an open country within fifty miles of their enemy's great capital, escape capture by the enemies which surrounded them, and keep forty thousand of their enemies back from the front actively and anxiously engaged in watching them: all this required pretty lively equestrian exercise."

As far as Mosby was concerned, his men could go without rations if necessary—he said he thought they fought better on empty stomachs—but the horses were to be fed and rested at any cost and at any sacrifice.

According to Munson, the majority of their horses came from captures in raids. "He (Mosby) divided all captured horses by lot among those who figured in the particular raid in which the animals were secured," Munson said. "Sutlers' supplies, army equipment and personal property belonged to the man brave enough to take the risk of capturing it."

Although the command was entitled to the spoils of war, Mosby never appropriated anything for himself. Even after the famous "Greenback Raid," in which his men captured $168,000 in Union payroll, Mosby ordered his name be struck from the list of those entitled to the prize-money. "Against this act of self-denial the men loudly protested, but to no purpose, for he is inexorable in his determination not to partake of the rich spoil which is daily captured by his command," Major John Scott wrote in his book *Partisan Life with Mosby*.

Munson reiterates that point. "Not a cent of this money went to Colonel Mosby. He paid his own way during the whole of his Partisan Ranger career out of his private means, buying his own horses and uniforms and everything he had."

## SOCIAL LIFE

Despite the many victories enjoyed by the command, no man could deny that riding with Mosby was a dangerous and perilous sport, his expeditions often ending with substantial loss, and seldom concluding without serious injury.

Still, the attractions far outweighed the hardships and risks, for the social life of the men belonging to this battalion was anything but inactive and mundane. In fact, as the command's reputation grew, so did the romance and mystique of those who were privileged enough to belong to it. Mosby's men were, by all accounts, the very aristocracy of the Confederate army and the honors lavished upon them by the inhabitants of Virginia were anything but disagreeable.

Consequently, for a Mosby man to spend half the night in the saddle skirmishing with the Yankees, and the other half engaged in social skirmishes with the opposite sex was an occurrence too common to be noted. To find a brightly lit home full of ladies with fluttering lashes and men with guns and spurs, while just outside stood horses ready to mount and commence an attack, was not deemed a bit out of the ordinary. To be dancing with a damsel one moment and be dancing with death the next, was a familiar, and by no means infrequent, affair.

According to young Munson, the men in Mosby's command enjoyed various diversions—horse races, card parties, and dances, principally. "The belles of Virginia were abundant and beaux were plentiful... There was not an unmarried man in Mosby's Confederacy who did not have one sweetheart at least, and some had more than their share."

Accordingly, there existed scarcely a parlor in Mosby's

Confederacy that was not regularly
invaded by "gentlemen" in muddy
boots and temporarily polished
manners. Mirth, music and soldier's
song would reign for hours and
the hearts of Virginia's finest ladies
would flutter with the chivalric
dignity so displayed. No little amount

of time was spent by these warriors informing the fair maidens
of the dangers and perils through which they had traversed on
Virginia's behalf, while not a little imagination was employed
to paint the scenes as vividly—and heroically, as possible.
Moreover no few hearts were left broken by the gallivanting
troopers who reveled in their legendary fame and distinction,
and used their worshipful status to their advantage when
dealing with members of the fairer sex.

It was because of this familiar relationship between citizens
and soldiers that a unique society developed, one which had a
marked effect among Mosby's men. This mingling of chivalry
and danger seemed to inspire the cavaliers with superb valor,
making them anxious to fight, willing to defend, and eager to
make the supreme sacrifice for their beloved countrymen...
and women.

Major Scott wrote that this unique association also served
as a way to keep the men in line. "Instead of the discipline
of camp, they are restrained by the discipline of society."
Mosby also kept order by making rules that Scott noted were
comprehensive and concise. The men knew they had to
"conduct themselves as soldiers on duty and as gentlemen off
duty."

This arrangement between the country folk and the command
had other benefits as well. When Union forces were in the
territory, which was not infrequently, details of conversations

overheard from Federal officers would find their way to Mosby, usually within moments of the words being spoken.

Scarcely would a plan be considered or a strategy conceived within the Federal ranks when it would be on its way to the rebel commander. Hence, Mosby knew the enemy's plans for movement and understood the condition and morale of the army. Likewise, he often knew the position of their pickets and even the schedule of their patrols.

Without the civilians and their close relationship with his command, Mosby's victories would not have been as prevalent or his triumphs as frequent. The cavalry officer relied heavily on the citizens of his territory and they, in turn, relied on his men to protect them from the brutality of the Union forces. No other commander could equal the respect or rapport that Mosby had built with the people in his region, and no amount of bribery, coercion, destruction of property or intimidation by Federal troops could compel the citizens to turn against him.

Dr. Monteiro wrote about the influence the officer had on the region. "Mosby exercised the most arbitrary power over his immediate command, and also over the several counties under his military control. He was considered not only a military ruler, but also a civil power of unquestioned authority, over the several counties known at that time as 'Mosby's Confederacy.' He settled all disputes, and his decisions admitted no appeal. If two old farmers quarreled about a horse trade, or the sale of real estate, the court of first appeal and last resort was the drum-head tribunal at Mosby's headquarters."

Edward Marshall, one of the most prominent and respectable citizens of Fauquier during the Civil War, goes a step further in stating Mosby's authority in the region. "Mosby has for nearly two years been king of Fauquier, and I have never known the county so well governed." (Quoted in Major John Scott's book *Partisan Life with Mosby*)

## TAKING THE LEAD

For his standing in the community and his valor on the battlefield, Mosby's men respected him, relying on his daring, his endurance, and his character, to get them out of any predicament. No one questioned his wisdom. No one doubted his courage. No one wavered in trusting their lives to his uncompromising sense of military honor and duty. He was regarded by them—and the enemy—as an incarnate genius of victory, one who manipulated the energy of war so as to render success certain.

Alexander wrote that Mosby knew each man personally, and, when meeting a new recruit, "seemed to read him at a glance and ascertain exactly what use to make of him." He mingled with his men, rode with them, slept with them, and fought side by side with them. "Few members of the command had a longer list of wounds and captures than himself," Alexander said. "His care against needlessly exposing them; his great skill in securing them every possible advantage; his cool, quiet courage, and the almost unvarying success of every enterprise which he personally conducted secured the perfect confidence of his men."

Many post-war writings from other military units bring up the conflicts and jealousies that existed between the men and their commanding officers. Not so with Mosby's men. It appears that those who served under him agreed that no leader in ancient or modern times ever possessed more cunning, more skill or more fearless intrepidity on the battlefield—nor more nobility, dignity or bearing off the battlefield, than Mosby.

Munson wrote, "Mosby's correct estimate of men, his absolute freedom from jealousy and selfishness, his unerring judgment at critical moments, his devotion to his men, his eternal vigilance, his unobtrusive bravery and his exalted sense of personal honor, all combined to create in the mind and hearts of those who served him a sort of hero worship."

Mosby's courage and judgment inspired his followers with such blind confidence that no endeavor was deemed impossible, or really even dangerous, as long as he was in command. He seemed to possess a mysterious power, a contagious energy that could move soldiers toward victory even without the use of words. The enemy often felt his resolve and the sway of his magnetic character when they watched certain victory seep from their grasp and flow triumphantly into his.

On the other hand, Mosby was not a person whom anyone would care to provoke. Those that knew him well, knew he was a solitary man, reserved and cautious, most at ease alone. He could ride for miles without speaking a word, and no man knew him well enough to guess with any accuracy what he would do next or how he would react to any particular circumstances.

Munson said that on the march Mosby was "usually very quiet and uncommunicative, riding by himself a little ahead of the command, apparently plunged in the consideration of some future problem. On a raid, however, when his mind was fully made up, he was the gayest of us all, joking and laughing with the men."

Tireless, relentless and seemingly always in the saddle, Mosby functioned as if impervious to danger and fatigue. Routinely returning from a fifty-mile scouting jaunt at sunrise, he would send out couriers to gather his men and return to the point of attack. No matter how many days he had been in the saddle, or how many hours since his last meal, he was capable of handling any challenge and overcoming any obstacle. Never, no matter the odds, did he hesitate or waver when commanding the field.

As one Southern newspaper wrote shortly after Mosby returned to duty after being seriously wounded:

"The indomitable and irrepressible Mosby is again in the saddle carrying destruction and consternation in his path. One day in Richmond wounded and eliciting the sympathy of every one capable of appreciating the daring deeds of the boldest and most successful partisan leader the war has produced—three days afterwards surprising and scattering a Yankee force at Salem as if they were frightened sheep fleeing before a hungry wolf—and then before the great mass of the people are made aware of the particulars of this dashing achievement, he has swooped around and cut the Baltimore and Ohio railroad, capturing a mail train and contents, and constituting himself, by virtue of the strength of his own right arm, and the keen blade it wields, a receiver of army funds for the United States. If he has not yet won a Brigadier's wreath upon his collar, the people have placed upon his brow one far more enduring."

*— Richmond Whig, October 18, 1864*

## SOME HUMOROUS ANECDOTES

Some said that Mosby was so successful because he had a way of processing information and then reacting with no hesitation. They compared the process to a bullet and the bang—one following the other so closely as to seem simultaneous.

Indeed, many of his exploits seem almost beyond the realm of possibility, to the extent that if they were written in a fictional plot they would be deemed unbelievable, implausible or at the very least, improbable.

For instance, in one close encounter with the enemy, Mosby took two Union troopers prisoner, and then rode straight through a Federal supply train with his captives rather than wait for it to pass.

Mosby wrote that after making the capture, he ran into the mile-long wagon train with a strong cavalry guard carrying supplies to the troops. After tying the halters of his prisoners' horses together so they could not run away, he drew his pistol, held it under cover, and told the prisoners that if they spoke a word they would be dead men.

"I then rode, with them by my side, through a gap in the fence into the pike, right among the Union cavalry. We went along for 200 yards, with my prisoners, through the wagon train and cavalry escort, until we got to a road leading away from the pike," Mosby wrote in his *Memoirs*. "The gum cloth I had over my shoulders to protect me from the rain, as it did not cover one-third of my body, did not conceal the uniform I wore. I had ridden through the ranks of a column of Union cavalry in broad daylight, with two prisoners, and my elbow had actually struck against one as I passed."

In another instance, Mosby used his quick wit to capture

five Yankees, again with no shots being fired. While he and his party were standing in front of a house, they saw in the starlight a squad of cavalry approaching from the direction of Winchester. When the enemy troops got within hailing distance they stopped and inquired of Mosby's party who they were.

John Alexander said that Mosby replied "'Friends, with the countersign,' with the best Yankee twang that he could improvise."

The enemy then yelled for one of Mosby's party to advance and give the countersign.

Alexander continues the story: "'No,' said the Colonel, 'you are coming from the direction of the enemy. One of you advance.'

"This was a correct proposition, so one of them rode forward. When he came up, the Colonel said to him in a low, terribly distinct voice, as he leveled his revolver at him: 'Give the alarm, and you are a dead man! I am Mosby. Now call to the others that it is all right, to come on.' And he did so; and five more of Uncle Sam's gallant defenders marched confidently up to the muzzles of as many revolvers and quietly surrendered."

But that is not the end of the story. According to Alexander, Mosby questioned the prisoners about their outpost (which he planned to attack), and then reported to his men.

"He told us, as a piece of good news," Alexander said, "that the picket had been reinforced that day, so that there were two hundred Yankees there instead of one hundred, as we first thought. And he added with a grim humor, 'Now we'll get two horses apiece instead of one.'"

Almost every one of Mosby's men relates in their memoirs a humorous story that occurred during the robbery of a train, later dubbed "The Greenback Raid." It seems that among the prisoners taken away was a young German lieutenant on his way to join the Yankees. When asked by Mosby why he had come over to fight against the Confederacy, the man replied, "Oh, I come to learn the art of war."

When Mosby ran across him again, the German's fancy overcoat, boots and hat had given way to a mixture of Federal and Rebel uniforms traded by his men. The German was furious and demanded his belongings be returned.

"Didn't you tell me you came to Virginia to learn the art of war?" Mosby asked.

"Yes, the German replied.

"Very well. This is your first lesson," Mosby replied as he rode away.

Another short anecdote involves Munson, who was riding a Yankee horse he had "recently acquired." Being closely pursued by Union forces while riding with two other Mosby men, he discovered with dismay that the horse was falling behind.

"The pursuers were then scarcely a hundred yards from me, and were calling to me in jeering tones between shots," he said. Just as his companions were riding away over the hill in the woods, he called out to them to stop and take him up on one of their horses. Instead, the two Mosby men wheeled and commenced firing at the Yankees.

Apparently the enemy had heard Munson yell, but didn't hear exactly what he had said. They also noticed that his horse had dropped to a quiet, dignified pace and assumed he was rallying his men for an ambush.

Munson says, "And I pledge to you my word of honor that the whole Federal party pulled up within almost touching distance of me and let me march in a quiet walk over the hill."

Yet another "raid" that shows the youth and exuberance of Mosby's command, occurred at Point of Rocks, just across the Potomac River from Virginia. After Mosby's men dislodged a Yankee force from the village in July of 1864, they began the work of plundering, first the camp, and then the stores.

"Most of the men went into the dry-goods business, and soon four regular shops and one sutler's establishment were emptied of their contents," said Major Scott.

Once the men had loaded themselves with everything they could bring off, Mosby ordered the command to re-cross the river.

Ranger John Alexander tells what happened after the men had cleaned out the stores.

"The gang that re-crossed the river that evening was a sight to behold. Bolts of cloth and calicoes were piled up behind and before them. Some of the latter, of gaudiest prints, served as sashes which streamed out from the shoulders or waists of the wearers; and yards upon yards of red and white bunting floated on the evening breeze. Boots and shoes hung from the saddles and the horses' necks; and various kinds of tin-ware flashed back the sunlight from every conceivable point of contact with a cavalier. The frequent presence of hoops and ladies' skirts and bonnets showed that the boys had not been unmindful of 'the girls they left behind them.'"

And Major Scott gives his version of events:

"Late in the evening the men resumed the march, bedecked in a very grotesque and original manner with their captured goods. As they passed along the road, some arrayed in crinoline, some wearing bonnets, and all disguised with some fantastic article of apparel, they looked like a company of masqueraders. Mrs. Dawson, who was in her garden as she beheld the strange procession drawing near, was seized with alarm, and, rushing to the house, exclaimed to her daughters, 'Run, my children, run to the garret! They are coming, they are coming! They ain't Yankees, and they ain't Rebs: they must be Indians!'"

Of course her fear turned into pleasure when she learned that they were only Mosby's men returning from what was dubbed, the "Calico Raid."

In December 1863, Mosby took the command to Brandy Station on the Orange and Alexandria Railroad, where he discovered part of a wagon train guarded by a brigade of infantry preparing to move. According to Crawford in *Mosby and his Men*, the wagon-master was riding up and down the train, hurriedly urging the teamsters to hurry up.

Crawford says that Mosby, with two men, rode up to the wagon-master, and complained about the delay of the train. "Mosby also rode through the guard while they stood around the fires with their arms stacked, and conversed with them in regard to the object of the movement of the army. He thus threw the enemy off their guard, representing his cavalry as the last of their rear-guard."

Returning to his command, Mosby placed himself at their head and moved them quietly to the wagons, which were standing some fifty yards from the numerous campfires. The men then proceeded to detach the mules and horses, and got out one hundred and twenty mules and ten horses before the enemy was aware of what he was doing.

"The first intimation they had of his doings was seeing the flames issuing from forty wagons which had been set on fire by the last of his men that left the train," Crawford said. "Before they could unstack their arms Mosby was out of their reach, with the mules and horses. They, however, fired one volley at him, without inflicting injury upon any one.

The mules were sent to General Lee, and the horses divided amongst the men."

In an even more successful raid that occurred right outside of Berryville, Va., Mosby's men discovered a long line of wagons that, according to Munson, could be heard long before they were seen.

"We rode among the drivers and the guards, looking the stock over and chatting with the men in a friendly way. I asked one of the cavalrymen for a match to light my pipe and he gave it to me, and when I struck it, revealing his face and mine by its light, he did not know I was pretty soon going to begin chasing him."

Munson goes on to describe the raid, which came to be known as the famous Berryville Raid. Mosby and his men came away with three hundred prisoners and nine hundred head of captured stock, including six hundred horses.

They burned more than one hundred wagons.

## THE END OF AN ERA

Mosby's Men were looking forward to more fighting in the spring of 1865 when suddenly Richmond fell, General Lee surrendered at Appomattox, and the curtain of war dropped on the last act.

According to Munson, Mosby and his men did not know of the surrender when they went into battle with the Eighth Illinois the following day, but he said after the war: "I sometimes feels sure that if we had known it was to be the last fight of our career, every man of us would have died rather than suffer the defeat that followed."

Dr. Monteiro recalled the moment that he showed Colonel Mosby the headline in a northern paper that Richmond had fallen. "The stern, brave, intrepid soldier gazed at the fatal lines that foretold the death of our country and our cause, and I gazed at him with the same intense feeling. When I saw tears gather in his eyes, I lost all hope."

Monteiro wrote of Mosby: "For years his whole heart had been wrapped in the fiery struggle for Southern liberty. No man ever offered up his life for any cause with more cheerful resignation than had our dauntless chief in hundreds of desperate conflicts."

The battalion was summoned for the last time by command of Colonel Mosby at Salem (now Marshall) in Fauquier County, to hear the farewell address of its brave and beloved commander.

According to Munson, no sadder ceremony ever occurred in the life of that little band of men, and, as Mosby rode along the line, looking each man in the face, it was plain that his heart was breaking.

Farewell Address:

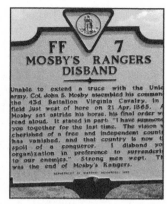

*Soldiers: I have summoned you together for the last time. The vision we cherished of a free and independent country has vanished, and that country is now the spoil of a conqueror. I disband your organization in preference to surrendering to our enemies. I am no longer your commander. After an association of more than two eventful years I part from you with a just pride in the fame of your achievements and grateful recollections of your generous kindness to myself. And now, at this moment of bidding you a final adieu, accept the assurance of my unchanging confidence and regard. Farewell!"*

Dr. Monteiro said this address was delivered in a voice tremulous with emotions of grief to eight hundred brave partisans, who listened "with bowed heads and moist eyes to the sad words that dissolved and severed forever the strong bonds that bound them to their gallant chief."

In his reflections about that day, Munson said that it wasn't possible for him to write an adequate description of the scene. "Singly and in groups, the participants in this saddest of farewells gave way to their feelings in a manner that requires no description. Strong men, who had laughed in the face of the gravest dangers and smiled at the pain of grievous wounds, walked apart to weep."

## HIS LEGEND LIVES ON

Born on Dec. 6, 1833, Mosby not only survived the war, but served as U.S. Consul to Hong Kong for seven years, from 1878-85. He later accepted a job with the Southern Pacific Railway, during which time he met a boy of about 10 years named George S. Patton, Jr. The story is often repeated that the old veteran shared some of the secrets of guerrilla warfare with the boy who would one day lead the 3rd U.S. Army into combat in Europe during World War II.

Mosby died in 1916 at the age of 82 and is buried in the Warrenton, Va., cemetery.

On June 19, 1920, a 25-foot granite monument was erected on the lawn beside the courthouse in Warrenton, Va. The inscription reads: "This tribute affectionately dedicated to Col. John S. Mosby, whose deeds of valor and heroic devotion to state and Southern principles are the pride and admiration of his soldier comrades and fellow countrymen. He has left a name that will live till honor, virtue, courage, all, shall cease to claim the homage of the heart."

Today, signs depicting a silhouetted horseman with a flag now mark the roads and byways of northern Virginia where Mosby once reigned. Loosely bound by the Bull Run Mountains to the east, the foothills of the Blue Ridge Mountains to the west, the Potomac River to the north and the Rappahannock River to the south, this scenic region, retains more than three centuries of its original historic landscape.

The beautiful vistas in this 1,800-square-mile section include dirt roads meandering over gently rolling hills, stone walls that stretch for miles, centuries-old mills and majestic homes.

Many of those homes still hold the secret trap doors that Mosby's Men used, and you can almost feel the presence of the Gray Ghost and his men staring down from the hillsides.

The Hathaway House in Mosby's Confederacy. Mosby once climbed out of the back window into the tree (pictured), to escape from a surprise visit by the Yankees in the middle of the night.

## To the Reader

THANK YOU FOR READING THIS BOOK on the life of Colonel John S. Mosby. I have enjoyed traveling the dirt roads of Virginia over the past 10 years so that I could attempt to bring to life a small piece of our nation's almost-forgotten history.

It is thrilling to stand on the very ground where Mosby stood, visit the houses where his men stayed, and walk the rolling hills where many of them fought and died.

Hopefully after reading this volume, you will share my passion for this amazing man and his group of ragtag followers, and will continue on a journey to learn more.

I urge you to visit the Mosby Heritage Area website, which I have included on the resources page, to find maps, timelines and additional historical information on the 43rd Virginia Cavalry.

Please stay tuned for other non-fiction releases that feature Forgotten American Heroes like Revolutionary War generals Francis Marion and Daniel Morgan.

You can find Jessica James here:

Jessica James Official Website
www.jessicajamesbooks.com
*(Use the Contact Me button on left to send an email)*

Jessica James *Life in the Past Lane* blog
www.jessicajamesblog.com

Jessica James Fan Page on Facebook
www.facebook.com/romantichistoricalfiction

Pinterest
www.pinterest.com/southernromance

@JessicaJames on Twitter

# Resources

The Mosby Heritage Area Association: www.mosbyheritagearea.org
Don Hakenson Author and Historian: www.hakenson.com

## Recommended Reads

This is by no means a comprehensive list, but includes many of
the volumes written by members of Mosby's command. There are
dozens of contemporary books on Mosby that are not listed here.

Alexander, John H., *Mosby's Men* (1907; reprint, Gaithersburg, Md.
1987)

Baird, Nancy Chappelear, ed., *Journals of Amanda Virginia Edmonds:
Lass of the Confederacy* 1859-1867 (Stephens City, Va., 1984). (Note:
Amanda's home was a "safe house" so her diary is an interesting
account of Mosby's men).

Crawford, John M., *Mosby and His Men* (New York, 1867)

Evans, Thomas J. and Moyer, James M., *Mosby's Confederacy: A Guide to
the Roads and Sites of Colonel John Singleton Mosby* (Shippensburg, 1991)

Hunter, Alexander, *The Women of the Debatable Land* (Washington,
1912)

Monteiro, Aristides, *War Reminiscences by the Surgeon of Mosby's Command* (1890; reprint, Gaithersburg, Md., no date)

Mitchell, Adele H., ed., *The Letters of John S. Mosby,* 2d ed., (no place,
1986).

Mosby, John S., *Mosby's War Reminiscences and Stuart's Cavalry Campaigns*
(New York, 1887)

Munson, John W., *Reminiscences of a Mosby Guerrilla* (1906; reprint,
Washington, D.C., 1983).

Russell, Charles W., ed., *The Memoirs of Colonel John S. Mosby* (1917;
reprint, Gaithersburg, Md., 1987)

Scott, John, *Partisan Life with Col. John Mosby* (1867; reprint Gaithersburg, Md., 1985)

Williamson, James J., *Mosby's Rangers* (1896; reprint, no place, 1982)

Made in United States
Orlando, FL
04 September 2022

21983853R00039